THE HEAT, THE HUSTLE & THE DRIVE

Life from a Basketball Mom's Perspective

ALISSIA MILES

THE HEAT, THE HUSTLE & THE DRIVE

Unless otherwise noted, all Bible quotations are from the King James Version of the Bible.

Cover: In Due Season Publishing ®

Editing and Interior Design Book Layout by
Enger Lanier Taylor for In Due Season Publishing ®

Published By: In Due Season Publishing ®
            Huntsville, Alabama
            indueseasonpublishing@gmail.com
            www.indueseasonpublishing.com

ISBN-13: 978-1-970057-30-0
ISBN-10: 1-970057-30-0

TABLE OF CONTENTS

Dedication

This book is dedicated to my loving husband, Tyshawn Miles, who encourages and pushes me to accomplish my goals.

To my darling children: Tyshawn Jr. (TJ), Malachi, Ariyana, Mathias, and Moriyah (RIH). Without y'all, Mommy would not be able to share her experiences or great wisdom. Thank you, babies!

To Coach Patrick, the idea of this book probably would not have happened if my boys were not a part of your basketball team. Thank you!

Introduction

Life as we know it can throw curve balls.
But even in the midst of that we must still
take heed to the call.
The call... What call?
The call that was spoken.
The call that was breathed into us.
Oh, please don't make a fuss!
Instead, just say hush when it comes.
When what comes?
The pressure...
Even when the pressure comes and
the temperature rises,
we must keep moving,
Hustling, and through the heat
We must keep driving.

Alissia Miles

Hi there! My name is Alissia Miles. I'm the wife to my wonderful husband, and the mother of four lovely children. Yes! My family. I love them dearly. Being a mom has been amazing, and so have the experiences that come with motherhood. Life in general, will cause us to be in a position to experience things to learn from and to grow. It just so happened that this book was written all because I was sitting and watching my boys at basketball practice. Hang tight! I will talk all about that momentarily. It is funny how you can get a whole message or revelation just watching something on television or while watching other people do things. That's what happened on the first day of practice. This book, "The Heat, The Hustle, & The Drive," is a basketball mom's perspective of life. These few basketball terms apply to how we live throughout life. I hope you are ready to view life from my shoes. Now bounce with me. (Ha!)

Chapter One
BRING ON THE HEAT

As I sit here and watch the children run up and down the court, I see the sweat dripping from their faces. I see them gasping for air. The children are tired and hot, but they must keep moving. I'm like wow...this is just the warm up of practice! My thoughts were, "Man, they have to work this hard in the warm up? Good Lord!" My boys had just joined the basketball league, and this was their first day of practice. I felt so sorry for them. I finally realized halfway through the practice that how they warm up was meant to build up their endurance in preparation for an actual game. You can practice shooting a basketball in different ways and from various spots on the court and be straight to play in a game. You can even practice defense and play all right in a game. However, that alone will not equip a player to last in a game. The warm-up, stretching, running up and down the court, quick feet, and skipping around will help a player build stamina when it is time to play in a game. I look at it as it's in the heat - doing the hard stuff that prepares you for the game. My sons' team name just so happened to be called "Xtreme Heat."

So, after just sitting here for a few minutes, I immediately started to think of this life and what it brings. THE HEAT! Trials and circumstances we face can bring a lot of heat. The heat causes us to sweat, lose our breath, and tire us out. Yes, we may get drained. We may get tired. We might even want to give up, but we must keep pushing. We must keep hustling, and we must keep driving.

The thing about trials is that no one is exempt. We all must go through something. As the seasoned folks say, "If you haven't been through nothing, then keep on living, baby." The trials we face are just a part of life. So, when it comes to trials, what really matters is 1) the hope one has to get through 2) the response, and 3) the growth. As a believer in Jesus Christ, I hope He will give me the strength to get through and overcome. My response should be no matter what I face; God is still God. No matter how hard it gets, I know I shall not be moved. I should also understand that whatever I go through it is to grow me up.

Hope

We should expect that even though it looks rough out here in these streets, we will overcome and be secure. There is a hope that we should have.

"Now faith brings our hopes into reality and becomes the foundation needed to acquire the things we long for. It is all the evidence required to prove what is still unseen."
Hebrews 11:1 (TPT)

Hope is the strong belief or desire for something to happen (Merriam-Webster). It is also a feeling of trust. What or who do you put your trust in? I put my trust in the Lord, for He can be trusted.

"Blessed [with spiritual security] is the man who believes and trusts in and relies on the LORD and whose hope and confident expectation is the LORD. For he will be [nourished] like a tree planted by the waters, That spreads out its roots by the river; And will not fear the heat when it comes; But it's leaves will be green and moist. And it will not be anxious and concerned in a year of drought nor stop bearing fruit."
Jeremiah 17:7 (AMP)

I like that part of scripture where it states "and will not fear the heat when it comes." We have security when we put our trust and lean totally on God. It is important to put our trust and hope in the Lord because when the heat comes, we will be able to stand firm like a tree planted by the water. The significant thing about being planted by the water is the tree roots spread to get the essential supply of nourishment which signifies the Word of God. To get the proper nutrition, we must become lovers of the Word of God and trust and rely on Him. That is what will sustain us when the heat comes. You will have nothing to fear.

The scripture also says that the tree leaves will be green and moist when the heat comes and bears much fruit during the drought. I love it! That is awesome to me. I won't dry out in the season of drought because I have consumed essential nutrients. There will be enough moisture to produce even in a dry season. It also says the leaves will be green. Green is a mixture of yellow and blue. Yellow signifies trials, and blue represents the Word of God. So, yellow and blue give you green – which signifies life or growth. So, blessed is the one that trusts and relies on the Lord.

Response

After having a hope in knowing that we are overcomers, we should also have a response like no other. Our attitude should be a little different. I remember a song that used to be the number one song a soloist would sing at a 3:00 pm service titled, *I Won't Complain*. Yes, it sounded so good. People would begin to rejoice and go into a praise break every single time, no matter who was singing it. Even in my youth, I would wonder if that statement was even true in the lives of those singing or hearing it.

In heated situations, what comes out of our mouths often does not reflect the actions or the response in our reality. We want to say I won't complain, but when it's not looking the way we want it to, or if it seems as if God has turned a deaf ear to our voice, we begin kicking, screaming, and having a tantrum like we're a toddler all over again. I understand that we are to speak those things which are not as though they are and that life and death are in the power of the tongue, but our actions and responses need to line up with the very words we professed out of our mouths when we are not in a room filled with people. By all means, continue to sing the song and encourage yourself, but let every word that flows out of your mouth be true and hold on to it.

Rejoice evermore. Pray without ceasing. In everything give thanks: for this is the will of God in Christ Jesus concerning you.
1 Thessalonians 5:16-18 (KJV)

The response that we are to have is to have a heart and a mind to rejoice, no matter what. Also, to embrace a life of prayer and to be thankful no matter what is going on in our lives because this is God's will for us. After having hope and a proper response, growth begins to occur.

Growth

My brethren, count it all joy when you fall into divers temptations, knowing this that the trying of your faith worketh patience. But let patience have her perfect work, that ye may be perfect and entire, wanting nothing.
James 1:2-4 (KJV)

So, when difficulties come, our faith is tested by the heat or the pressure that builds our endurance. According to the text, our response is to count it all joy when we face trials.? Because it is an open door to encounter the greatest joy possible, knowing that this trial is not to kill me but it is to groom me. It is to prepare and to teach me. It is to grow me up. When my faith is tested, the power of endurance springs forth in me and grows stronger, which will cause me to be strengthened and perfected into every part of my being. Thank you, Jesus!

Personal Testimony

There was a time in my life when I experienced heat in a way I never had before. I was pregnant with my fourth child, and we were informed of an issue concerning her heart in the fifth month. She was diagnosed with Tetralogy of Fallot. I was familiar with the term because my nephew experienced this when he was an infant. It is basically a condition that consists of four defects of the heart that causes poor blood flow from the heart (Mayo Clinic). This was a serious matter because, at the time of delivery, they had many people in place to take her if emergency surgery was needed. Thankfully, it was not required. So, I had little time to hold my sweet baby when she was born. I named her Moriyah because it means "The Lord is my Teacher." I wanted the Lord to guide her as she walked through this life. However, that was not the case. The Lord switched that thing around. He had to teach me a few things through my daughter's life.

She had to stay in the hospital for the first four months of her life. The pressure was real for us during that time. We had three small children in Pre-K, Kindergarten, and the oldest in second grade. There was a 30-minute commute to the hospital every day. There were days we couldn't make it because we did not have enough gas in the car or not enough to pay for parking. Our hearts were crushed because we felt horrible on the days we couldn't get to her. Then on top of that, we had to manage what we had to do weekly at church.

At the time, my husband was the only one working, and he was going to school full-time as well. It was a lot to manage. It seemed like we had to deal with something new almost every week with my daughter, as if the heat kept intensifying. We would hear, "Oh...she has what we call DiGeorge Syndrome, which has affected the muscles in her mouth to be weakened to the point where she cannot be breastfed or drink from a bottle. So, we have to give her a feeding tube through her nose and work our way up to a G-tube. Oh...she is not getting enough air, so we must do a procedure to balloon the air passageway." It felt like our baby was never coming home. Then it was, "Oh...she now has an infection because of the length of time the IV has been in her vein." The list could go on and on.

As a mom, I felt more and more helpless each day. There was literally nothing I could do. At certain times she was hooked up to so many tubes I couldn't even hold my sweet girl. That was what crushed me the most. You know when your child needs momma, but I couldn't even wrap my arms around her. So, what do I do? I sing! I can't hold you like I want to, but you will know Mommy is right here.

In the uncomfortable and struggling moments Moriyah had, all I could do was sing. When she heard my voice, she would instantly calm down. I remember this one time I walked in her room and went straight to the sink to wash my hands. She immediately knew I was in the room. She started crying and shaking her head as if she was trying to tell me something. I walked over to the side of her bed. She was hooked up to so many tubes and had the oxygen mask over her little nose, and she just kept shaking her head. I was questioning in my head, "What is going on up in here?" I called the nurse to let her know that my baby seemed very uncomfortable and that she would not stop shaking her head. Of course, there was nothing the nurse could do. I just stood there, lost as to what I could do. My baby looked at me with tears flowing down her angelic face. She still shook her head as if telling me she was still fighting. She was crying. I was crying. I was like,

Lord, "What do I do?" So, I sat down in the chair, pulled out my phone, and began to play a song I had to sing on Sunday. It was called "Holy Spirit, You Are Welcome, Here." I sat there crying and singing the song as my prayer for that moment. I said, "Lord there is nothing I can do, so I welcome you right here and now in this present moment."

I noticed that Moriyah started to calm down. I put the song on repeat and kept on singing. I noticed a peace in the room, and she was no longer shaking her little head. Then I started to calm down as she was now drifting off to sleep. The Chaplain was doing her rounds and entered the room. She was stunned when she came in. She heard the music playing and asked, "Do you know what you just did here?" She said, "You just shifted this whole atmosphere, and it is so peaceful here. Truly the presence of the Lord is in this room." She walked out, and all I could say was, "Thank you, Lord." I was so grateful that the Lord was on the scene. There was nothing I could have done, but I called on the name of the Lord, and He definitely heard my cry and let me know that He was right there. To this very day, that song is my favorite and one of my "go-to's" when I don't know what to sing. I want to become more aware of His presence in the midst of whatever I may face. I want to experience the glory of His goodness. God is so good and worthy of everything I can give, even in the midst of every hardship. I wish I had that mindset during that time.

In the whole process of what we had to deal with in the life of my sweet baby Moriyah, sometimes I felt like I could hold on to God and His Word, but then there were times I was like, "Okay, God, anytime you want to step in that would be great." There were times that I failed to realize that every day Moriyah was breathing, that was God at work. Every day that I could see her was God at work. The effect she had on all the nurses was God at work. To make a long story short, Moriyah lived eight months here on this earth. Throughout that whole process, her little life touched the lives of all who cared for her. The impact this baby had was amazing. There were moments in our alone time with her that we would be interrupted because nurses would just pop their heads in to see and love on her. That would bother me because I was like, "Don't you see us here trying to enjoy the time we have with our daughter?" My husband wasn't bothered by it. He shifted his perspective. He told me that people were attracted to her because she was being used for God's glory. This child had to be here because some years prior, I had a procedure done that would permanently stop me from having more babies. We were told that the procedure failed, and the funny thing was on the day, I was scheduled for a tubal ligation. They said, "Not so. You are too late. You're already pregnant, ma'am." I learned that God has a sense of humor.

So, the challenges and pressures we had experienced had taught me a lot. As stated earlier, the Lord had to really teach me some things. I had to grow in a lot of areas. What I was professing I really wasn't living. The Jesus I sang about I really didn't know. The things I knew about God were just surface level stuff. I really didn't have a solid relationship with Him. It was at that moment I had to forget everything I was taught and everything I knew. I had to learn Jesus all over again. I had to truly get to know him for myself, not through the words of my parents or from other people, but from my own experience. I am so glad to say that I did. It was through the greatest heat I have ever experienced where my faith was being tested, and endurance was being perfected in me to allow me to grow in what God needed to do through me. So, now when I look around and think things over, I can honestly say, I won't complain.

Just for memory's sake, here are the lyrics to, *I Won't Complain*, by Rev. Paul Jones:

I've had some good days.
I've had some hills to climb
I've had some weary days and
some sleepless nights
But when I look around, and I
think things over
All of my good days outweigh my
bad days I won't complain
Sometimes the clouds hang low.
I can hardly see the road.
I ask a question, Lord, why so much pain?
But He knows what's best for me.
Although my weary eyes they can't see
So, I'll just say thank You, Lord
I won't complain.
The Lord has been so good to me.
He's been good to me
More than this whole world or you
could ever be.
He's been so good to me
He dried all of my tears away
Turned my midnights into day
So, I'll just say thank you, Lord.
I won't complain.

Now take a moment to reflect.....

When heat or pressure comes, how do you respond? After reading the scriptures in this passage, how should you respond?

_____

_____

_____

_____

_____

_____

_____

_____

_____

_____

_____

_____

Write down a time where you experienced growth from a situation that brought on some heat and begin to thank God for what He has done.

_____

_____

_____

_____

_____

_____

Chapter Two
I'M ON FIRE

The heat... "Heating up refers to when a player has made a number of shots in a row during a stretch of time in a game. This is the player who has a better chance of making a basket (Sports Lingo)."

The Heat references the player who has a better chance of making the basket. Yes, you, my dear friend, are always in the heat of the game. I don't know if you ever played basketball video games, but this reminds me of one in particular. When your player was in the heat of the game, the announcer would say, "He's on Fire!" At that moment, the player seemed unstoppable and able to make every shot. So yeah, you are on fire! You are most likely to get called on for everything. You are the one with a better chance of making it all happen. You are the one that everyone is looking at. Your job is calling for you. Your children are calling for you. Your church community is calling for you. People you don't know are calling and looking for you because you are filled with something they need.

Mothers, fathers, wives, and husbands all have a great responsibility. Mothers, you are called to nurture and diligently teach your children. Wives, you are called to help, respect, and submit to your husbands as you do to the Lord. Husbands, you are called to be the head of the household, love your wives just as Christ loved the church, honor your wife, treat her with understanding, and enjoy life with her. Fathers, you are called to protect your children and bring them up in the discipline and instruction of the Lord. Guess what, people?! We are all called to serve. We are called to something. We are called to action. We are called to be impactful in our homes, children's lives, places of work, and everywhere we go.

You are the one who has a better chance to make the basket because you were called to do it. I know that you probably have a lot going on in your life. Pressure coming from here, pressure coming from there, here pressure, there pressure, everywhere pressure! I get it. Trust me, I get it. However, with the busyness this life brings, we cannot afford to get distracted and lose sight of what matters. We must work, but our responsibilities to our families cannot go lacking. We must take care of business, but our responsibility as a believer cannot go lacking either. We have church obligations, but our community cannot go lacking either.

As the basketball players on the court have to look at the clock to carry out the plays in a certain amount of time, we must do the same. We have a number of plays (dreams, goals, ideas, kingdom assignments) that we want to make sure happens before the clock runs out. So, that means we must manage our time wisely, plan accordingly to fit everything and everyone into our lovely schedules. We must start with God at the center of it all. He will then give us instructions to align us on how to bring balance to every area of our lives.

Impactful

I wanted to return to the abovementioned statement about how we are called to be impactful. What does it mean to be impactful? It means to produce a marked impression (Merriam-Webster). As long as you are still breathing, you are to be impactful. I am here to tell you that it is time to make your mark if you haven't already. Making an impact may not look the same for everyone. For some, you may make an impact and change the lives of 500,000 people. For some, you may impact one life that will forever be changed because you took the time to pour into that person's life. It does not matter how many you impact, but how you use your influence. The whole point is whoever you come in contact with; there should be a noticeable marked impression because there was a noticeable change within that individual.

I look at it this way, letting your light so shine before men that they may see your good works and glorify your Father in heaven according to Matthew 5:16 (NKJV). Let Him be glorified with your life.

Impacting the Family

As previously stated, parents are responsible for impacting their children's lives. It is vital, especially today when there has been such a heavy attack on children. The devil's schemes have been aggressive toward them. Many are confused and lost when it comes to their identity. They have no clue that they are fearfully and wonderfully made. They have no idea that there is something unique and powerful that is deep within them. Many have been faced with great pressure, which is bothersome because it has led to depression, drugs, violence, and suicide. Many are bullied by their parents, which has molded their minds to react the same and bully their

THE HEAT, THE HUSTLE & THE DRIVE

peers. Then to top it all off, the demonic systems of this world are trying to get rid of them before they even exit the womb. So what are we going to do about it? Parents, we cannot neglect our children because we are too busy focusing on other things, which now leaves our children left out, and as a target for being groomed by worldly influences. Not so! It is high time to start managing our lives so nothing becomes lacking. Your children need you. What they receive from you will carry them throughout their whole lives. So be very careful of what you let them see. Be very careful of what you let them hear. Be very careful of how you treat them. Ask the Holy Spirit to teach you the things that you do not know concerning parenting.

Maybe you did not have a father or mother figure, which has left you lost. I guarantee if you seek the Holy Spirit, He will guide you. He will give you the wisdom on how to parent your children. It is time to be the example your children need. Don't allow society to show them. Don't let the systems of this world show them. Teach your daughters what it means to be feminine and what true beauty looks like. Teach your sons what masculinity is all about and how to carry themselves. Teach your children what it means to have a heart after God. Teach them what it means to deny ungodliness and worldly lusts.

Teach them what living soberly and godly means in this world. Let it be ever on the forefront of your mind. Ask the Holy Spirit to help you to be a positive example in their lives. Encourage them to go after their heart's desire and not be afraid. Let them know that they are on the earth to fulfill their purpose. Let them know that they are created in the image and likeness of God, and their true identity is found in Him.

Impacting the Community

Being involved in the community can make a huge difference in the lives of many. It is time for the church (which consists of the people) to be a church without walls. Wherever we go and whatever we do, we represent the church. What does it look like to be a church without walls and being the hands and feet of Jesus? I'm reminded of a song by Casting Crowns entitled "If We Are the Body." You should listen to it when you get a chance. The lyrics say, "If we are the body, why aren't His hands reaching? Why aren't His hands healing? Why aren't His words teaching?" In the time we are living in with all we have experienced in the pandemic, this is the right moment for the people of God to be in place to reach out to the community. This is the right moment for the house of God to be the storehouse for our communities. This is the time to be impactful.

As Jesus walked the earth, He impacted the lives He encountered, and He served. Their lives were changed forever. They were instantly healed, delivered, and set free.

I have made it my daily prayer. Every morning while driving into work at this one particular corner, the sun shines so brightly on my face, and I will say, "Lord, as the sun is shining on my face, I ask that you shine on and through me this very day so that whoever I come in contact with can see you. "Let there be an opportunity to share Jesus with someone today; however, that may look like here in the workplace." Then guess what? The opportunity was always there. When the opportunity presented itself, I had to choose to move. There were many times I was hesitant, but I didn't let that stop me all because I was at work. I saw how severely people needed someone to pour into them. They needed a listening ear. They needed encouragement. They were seeking help. They needed Jesus. It is my desire wherever I go to share the love of Jesus.

Personal Testimony

So, about a year after the passing of my sweet baby girl, I had the opportunity to make an impact into the life of a mother who lost her baby girl, as well, in a similar situation. I did not know her at all. My good friend called me one day explaining the lady's situation, and she said that I was the first person that came to her mind. My friend reached out to me because she knew I had a story and knew I could make an impact. At first, I was like, "Alright, Lord, how will I do this? What am I going to say? How do I go about this?" This lady did not speak English, so we were trying to figure out if we needed to do something like a video chat and my friend could interpret for me. The lady turned that down because she was in a state of grief where she couldn't even bear to talk about it. She was a new believer in Christ and was starting to have doubts because she could not understand how this could happen. I began to pray and ask God how I could encourage her. I asked Him for the right words and the right timing. I waited a few days in order to get direction on how to respond. I then asked for the lady's email address and began to write. I began to empathize and share a little bit of my story.

I did not let the barrier of communication stop me because I did not speak Spanish. After writing the email, I copied and pasted what I wrote and put it in Google translation to convert my English into Spanish. I sent the email, hoping for a response. Months went by and I didn't receive a response. I hoped and prayed that what I shared was impactful. I reached out to my friend as time went by asking if she had heard from the lady. She said she did and stated that what I wrote really helped her. She said she apologized for not responding, but she was still in shock. However, she was very thankful for me sharing my experience with her.

About a year and a half later, my friend reached back out to me to let me know that she had heard from the lady and wanted to give me an update. She said that she was doing well and that she was expecting another bundle of joy. I was so excited to hear the great news! She also stated that she was a little nervous about the pregnancy. It was then I felt like I needed to write to her again to go a little deeper into my story. The first time I reached out to her, I just shared some encouraging words, and how I came out on the other side of grief, and that was it. This time, I shared the miracle God performed in my life with her. Allow me to share with you what I shared with her. I began to share how I could not have another child scientifically after losing my baby girl. Yes, I made sure to schedule a tubal removal procedure six weeks after delivery. I wasn't playing any more games. You hear me! I was cool with that, but God had other plans. I remember I was feeling a little different, and my husband kept saying, "Baby, you're glowing." Every time he would say that I already knew the deal. I realized that I was a week late on my cycle. So, I went and took a pregnancy test. I was so nervous waiting for the results. It turned out to be positive, and all I could do was cry. At that point in time, I was still grieving, so it was hard for me to embrace what was happening. I didn't want to share with anyone because I wanted to see a doctor first. My husband knew all along, so he was excited. I made an appointment to see my doctor, but she had a full schedule and couldn't see me, so I had to see another doctor. I was upset because I didn't want to see anyone else. I wanted to see my doctor to tell her she had screwed up again. I laugh now, but that's what I wanted to say to her, even though I knew she had nothing to do with it. We went to see this other doctor whom I was very uncomfortable seeing from the jump. He viewed the pictures from the ultrasound and informed us that my hormone levels for being pregnant were high. However, there was no fetus in the sac. So, during this visit, he was trying to say that I may have an ectopic pregnancy. He also stated that if I were his patient, he would recommend that I terminate the pregnancy, or it could be detrimental to my health. He kept saying that over and over, and it was like the more he said it, I completely tuned him out. I turned the volume down on him because he pointed out a little speck in the sac that didn't appear to be a fetus, but maybe a speck of blood. Once he said that I didn't want to hear anything else he had to say. The fact that something was there gave me hope, and the fact that he said it was blood gave me some more hope because in my head, I was thinking about the blood of Jesus being applied over this situation (Where my churchy folks at?).

At that moment, I remembered that I had received a prophetic word a week prior from a good friend saying, "During this next test, it is your faith in God that is going to get you through." She had no clue of my situation, so I held on to those words. Now back to that moment... I held on to my faith in God because I truly believed a fetus existed in that sac. I didn't care if it didn't look like a fetus, but because something was there, I was uncomfortable with letting that slide. I told the doctor, "You know what? We'll just wait it out." It was like the more we said we'd wait, the more he pushed his thoughts on us about terminating this pregnancy. I kept hearing, "If you were my patient, I would go in for emergency surgery to terminate because although I don't see anything on your fallopian tubes, you have a cyst there that is blocking our view." So, you mean to tell me that you are unsure about nothing and want me to do what? I really felt that this was a setup straight from hell to get me to terminate the miracle that was happening. He finally dropped his point of view and recommended that I take it easy over the weekend and, if I were to start feeling lightheaded or in pain, to immediately come in because this can be detrimental to my health. The very next day, it was like I couldn't get that doctor's words out of my head. As I was sitting there folding clothes, I started feeling "off" in my body, and as I got up to go upstairs, I almost fell over because I was lightheaded. I immediately questioned my decision!

What he said may have been right. My husband said, "Let's go to the emergency room and get you checked out to be on the safe side." So, we were there in the emergency room explaining what was going on and what we had heard the day before from the doctor. They wanted to do an ultrasound, and after viewing it, what do you know they came back saying? You're PREGNANT, and there is a fetus in the sac. Well, just take my breath away! I was one excited and furious person all at the same time. I said I'd better not ever see that doctor again. Then I realized that this was the test I had received word about. I was glad I held on to my faith in God and what He was capable of. I was still grieving the loss of Moriyah. That's why I was upset when I found out we weren't having a girl, but I believed this bundle of joy helped me through the grieving process. He is our gift from God, which is why I named him Mathias.

Now take a moment to reflect.......

Can you remember when you made a marked impression in the community, workplace, or an individual's life? If not, do you see an opportunity presently to do so? If so, explain and then try to make your mark. If not, ask God to present that opportunity before you and use you to make a marked impression in someone's life, for He will do it.

_____

_____

_____

_____

_____

_____

Chapter Three
GET OFF THE BENCH

Phwwwwhhtt (whistle blows)! Malachi, you're in!" Yep, that's my boy getting called into the game. He jumps right up and hustles into his rightful position on the court. Yeah, man, he's ready to play. He worked his butt off for this moment and has put in the time and dedication in practice. Even though some of his teammates talked about him and told him, he wasn't good enough. He could have decided to tell his coach that he wasn't ready. He could have even said that he wasn't feeling it today. He could have also told his coach that he was scared or didn't feel like he was the right player for the moment. He owned the moment and understood what he had prepared himself for in practice. He made the choice to get off the bench.

In life, we are going to be called off the bench whether we want to be or not. It can be for many different reasons. At this very moment, you may be getting called off the bench because you are trying to go after your dreams and you simply cannot remain stuck in a place of complacency. You could be getting called off the bench because you are needing a change in your life, and that change has to begin with you. You may be getting called off the bench because fear has paralyzed you and you must face this giant in order to bring it down. Whatever the reason for you remaining on the bench and refusing to get in the game, now is the time to make up your mind and say, "Hey let me in, Coach. I'm ready to get off the bench and play." Use those skills, the dominion, and the authority that you have already been graced with that was breathed into you way before when you were in your mother's womb.

It is time to come out of hiding and rise to the occasion. You have been blessed with beautiful gifts and skills that will get you to the places you couldn't have even imagined. God has placed things inside of you so when you release it into the earth it brings Him glory. You may be in a place where you have been at a standstill, or you have let things block you from getting to the next place. When you do not know who you are and what lies within you, it prevents you from operating at your full capacity. It is time to tap into what God has placed on the inside of you and begin to command it to come forth.

Overload of Greatness

One day my husband's friend contacted him and gave him a message concerning me. He said he was praying for me because there was an overload of greatness inside me. I agreed with what he said. I knew I had a lot of gifts and creativity inside of me, just bubbling over and ready to be released. Have you ever been so frustrated because you know you have a lot to offer, but you don't really know where to start? Then frustration sets in, and you push those thoughts to the side. I was in that space. It seemed as if when I would try to get up and do something, a big, huge heavy door slammed right in my face. Disappointment would set in because I knew I should be doing something, but it always seemed to get blocked. So, I gave up on what I was working on, and went back to doing nothing. Sometime after, I was at a point where I realized that God had placed many things in me that must be accomplished, and I did not know where to start. What do You want me to do right now? It wasn't until I sat down and focused and sought after what God wanted me to focus on first. Yes, I was full of great things, but I realized that there is a timing for each one.

After I sought the Lord for what was next in my life, it was a few days later, while I was at a consecration elevation service at my church, the Lord spoke to the man of God who was speaking, and the words given to me were to "WRITE THE BOOK." At that time, I was in the beginning stages of writing this book, unsure how it would all come together, but after receiving those words, everything became clear. So, I was on a mission to get off the bench and heed the instruction to start writing.

I am not the only one filled with an overload of greatness. You are too! There is greatness inside of you, and it has been there all along. If you are feeling the way I was, I admonish you to get in a quiet space and chat with the Lord. Trust and believe whatever He says because it was already planned from the beginning.

Personal Testimony

I wish I could say getting off the bench was that simple, but it wasn't. It took me a long time. You know, there were moments when I thought I was ready to get off the bench, and did. However, I didn't have to get called out of the game. Due to fear and feeling inadequate, I sat *myself* back down on the bench and said, "Nope, not doing it." Looking back now, I'm like, "Girl, why didn't you, or you should have done this." Although I can't go back and do it all over again, I did learn from those moments. I realized

I was the one standing in the way of me going further. I hated being in my own way.

Many years ago, fear gripped me so that when I finally broke free, I realized I was tripping for nothing. Oh, my goodness! When I graduated from high school and was preparing for college, I didn't know what to expect. I did not know much about the Internet and sending emails then. A few of my classes were set up for our assignments to be submitted via email. I had no clue and was too scared to ask for help. On top of that, my advisor put me in the most challenging classes in my first semester. So I dropped out of school because I was afraid to open up my mouth to get the assistance I needed and thought it was too hard. So, I gave up. I quit. I had some regrets. I felt like a total failure. I was mad at myself because there was no good reason why I was sitting there wishing something good could come my way. I was too scared to go to school. I was afraid to find a job. Not that I didn't want to work. I was terrified of the thought of having an interview. I am a straight-up introvert. I don't like talking to anybody. So, the thought of having to answer questions correctly and telling people why I thought I was a good fit for the position just scared me. I still didn't have a clue. So, time went on, and I finally got the courage to apply for a job. There was a little while until I got married and had to move. Even meeting and getting married to my husband was a miracle because he had to pull teeth to get me to talk to him. The Lord sho' nuff had to be working. As time passed, babies were on the scene (We didn't waste any time). I still wanted to accomplish my goal of returning to school. I was a stay-at-home mom for years. I wanted to work, but my children were young at the time and not in school, which meant daycare costs would have been extremely high.

I researched several universities that offered flexible hours for busy people. I finally found one and signed up to get a call back from a representative. I finally answered the phone because I knew they would keep calling if I didn't. The representative's greeting was kind and warm. She briefly introduced me to the school and asked me all these questions. I rolled my eyes again because I didn't like a lot of questions, although I kindly answered them. Then she asked, "What held you back all these years?" It was then that everything seemed to stop, and I had to look at myself and what I was doing or not doing for all these years.

The waterworks began and I started to cry hysterically. I couldn't even answer the question. It probably took me five minutes, although it felt like 10 minutes to answer the question. This lady thought that something traumatic had happened to me. It's funny to me now, but it wasn't funny on that call. I finally told her I wasn't successful on the first attempt and felt like a failure. I expressed how I wanted to do something about it. She calmed me down, and I'll never forget what she said. She said, "It seems to me that fear is holding you back, and you need to face and overcome it." She was calling me off the bench. I agreed and told her to sign me up before I changed my mind.

I am glad to say that I, Alissia Miles, a mother of three children (preparing for the fourth at that time), graduated and received a Bachelor of Science in Business Management. It was one of the proudest moments in my life. I went back to school just to overcome fear and prove that I could do anything I put my mind to doing. No, I wasn't searching for a career, and people did not understand why. They would say I had this degree and wasn't doing anything with it. It may have seemed like I was doing nothing to them, but I accomplished my goal. I had overcome fear. I am now an example to my children: when you want to give up, feel like you have failed, or are too scared to pursue things right at your fingertips, please get off the bench and rerun the play!

Now take a moment to reflect...

Is there an area in your life where you are being called off the bench and ready to say, "Let me in, coach. I'm ready to play?" If so, jot down those areas and what your course of action will be to achieve those goals.

_____

_____

_____

_____

_____

_____

_____

_____

_____

_____

_____

_____

_____

_____

_____

_____

_____

_____

_____

Chapter Four
PLAY HARD

The hustle... "playing hard and providing great effort consistently to win (Basketball Society)."

"Go hard or go home!" Playing hard or providing great effort is definitely a part of our everyday lives. Whether it's playing hard to ensure food is on the table, accomplishing what we view as great success, impacting your children's lives, or just staying sane. Guess what? It all takes great effort. Diligence is key. We all want to make it. We all want to win. Please understand that everyone's win will not look the same as yours, which is okay. What you value as of utmost importance, someone else will not. So in those times when you may face opposition because others may not understand what game you are in and trying to win, diligence will have to be a vital characteristic you possess.

Here is a perfect example: I love the game of basketball. I couldn't wait to get to middle school just to play, although my dreams were shattered due to having surgery on my left hip. My little ole' feelings were hurt. Anyway, I love and have an understanding of the game. I like it so much that even though my boys are on a team, I also cheer for the opposite team when they make a smooth play. I'll just start hollering. Yeah, I'm that mom, and that wife who her husband does not want to sit by at the game. The point I am trying to make is that I will cheer you on when you're playing a game that I understand. Now with football, you won't get many screams out of me. I don't care for football, and I hate sitting there for an extended period of time just looking at boys pushing people down. So, I guess I need to learn the game since my boys think they ought to play football too. Lord help! I don't fully understand the game of football or why my boys feel like they must play that as well. However, that doesn't give me the right to tear down their dreams of playing.

I will still show my support. Now I may not know a lot about football, but one thing I do know is that there is an end zone that players definitely want to cross, and when they do, there is a burst of applause, jumping, and screaming. No, I don't necessarily care for the game, but when my baby or his teammate crosses the end zone, you better know I am going to raise up and clap my hands and scream. I'll even cheer for the other team because if you are pushing through all that body weight trying to stop you and block you from getting to where you are going, you definitely impressed me. Good ole' Mother Miles will applaud you. I said all this because I encourage you to keep pushing, my dear friend. If you do not have people in your corner cheering you on, please surround yourself with people that care about your win, even if they don't quite understand what you are doing.

You deserve that! If you don't have that, please read my words and imagine me speaking directly to you: ma'am, sir, young lady, young man, whoever you are, you've got this! Whatever your vision, dreams, and goals are, don't stop pushing. Don't stop hustling. This is the call to diligence for you. I don't care if you feel like you have failed. I don't care if you feel like you have wasted a lot of time. I don't care if you have given up on your win. Hear me today, GET UP, and forget those things which are behind you. Push through all the heavyweight and the obstacles that may be in front of you and get to hustling, baby!

The Call to Diligence

The Cambridge Dictionary defines *diligence* as careful work done with great effort or energy, which is to do something with showing thought and close attention to your actions. It is being cautious of the task at hand. Ask yourself if this is something you need to be doing right now or if this task distracts you from getting to where you need to go. Diligence is that persistent work where you continue in that thing despite difficulty or opposition. Diligence continues to endure over a long period of time. You may not immediately see the results of your labor, but the diligent one will continue to endure until they see the manifestation. We all must work. No one is exempt. That is just the way it is. How we manage our work truly matters.

Characteristics

A diligent person has specific characteristics that distinguish them. One would value the precious commodity called time. Diligent people are wise with their time. When it comes to deadlines and appointments, they are on time and take them seriously. Another characteristic would be to persevere through challenging tasks without complaining and have a mind to keep learning to improve the skills they already possess. A diligent person will have a bounce-back mentality if things don't go as planned and will find another way to make it happen.

So, if no one pushes you, you must learn to motivate and encourage yourself. You have to know the value of what you offer; because you know you are valuable, you will do whatever it takes to persistently work to accomplish what you desire. The diligent person understands that every day matters. It is important for you to live with purpose and to be intentional in what you are doing in your life. We are allowed to make our mark on the earth with each day that we are given. It is important to be awakened to the call to diligence because you will face opposition; for there is an opponent, or should I say an enemy trying to block you from getting to where you are destined to go. You must **F**ollow. **O**ne. **C**ourse. **U**ntil. **S**uccessful (Thank you, Pastor Brad)! You will need to be so focused and driven that you will know when it is time to perform a change-of-pace to dribble past your opponent, so you can shoot and hit nothing but the net.

Now take a moment to reflect...

Take some time to read Proverbs 30:25-26, Proverbs 28:19, and Proverbs 6:6-8. Based on the scriptures, jot down your thoughts on the importance of diligence and hard work. Also, jot down how you can be more diligent in accomplishing the things you desire.

_____
_____
_____
_____
_____
_____
_____
_____
_____
_____
_____
_____
_____
_____
_____
_____
_____
_____
_____
_____
_____

Chapter Five
WATCH ME MOVE

The drive... "an aggressive move toward the basket by a player with the intention of scoring."
–Greg Hawk

My dear friends moving rapidly with purpose and with your God-given authority is important for the remaining days of your life. We have all been called and appointed by the Coach to play in this game called life. No, we did not have to try out. We were automatically drafted to be on a team. There are no if's, and's, or but's about it. God called and chose us to be present on this earth for a purpose. It was already destined. You must become aware of and complete some assignments inside of you. God wants His people to arise on the scene and move rapidly to fulfill their original purpose for being placed on the earth. I do not know what you have been called to do, but I can say that you have the ball in your hand, and it is time to make your way to the basket and score. We are constantly moving toward the "American Dream," not to say anything is wrong with that. However, when we realize the reason we are here on the earth, our mindsets will shift on purpose. Our purpose is for God to get the glory out of our lives. We are to reach out and touch the lives that we are surrounded by. We are to give the people Jesus. We reach people with what we were created to do.

When God has given you the play, it is so crucial that you drive. God does not leave us out here lost or confused. He will send you instructions on what you are to do and how to do it. I am reminded of Noah in the Bible. God gave him specific instructions on how to build the Ark. He left nothing out. He told him why He wanted him to build it. He told him what materials to use and the exact measurements. I also like reading about Abraham in the Bible when God instructed him to go to a place "Where I will send you." He left his kindred and the place of familiarity to go where God wanted him to be.

I wonder what his thoughts were when he heard those instructions. I wonder if he was scared or hesitant to move. I wonder if he questioned God as to why he must go and leave everything. It doesn't make sense. You may not get all the information at once, but you'll receive the instructions for the first step, and you drive and complete step one; then the next step will come after. When you receive instructions and do not obey, it shows your lack of trust in the Lord. God is not going to tell you to do something that does not have a purpose. So, that means everything will be lined out or planned out for you to be successful with whatever he told you to do. Do you trust God with your life? Trust means believing in the reliability, ability, truth, and strength in someone or something (Merriam-Webster). Can you honestly say that you firmly believe in God's reliability and His ability? Can you honestly say you have a firm belief in the truth and the strength of God? I must say that I have not always had that firm belief in the God that I serve, but maturing and making a choice to go deeper into the Word of God and to gain an understanding of who He is was life-changing for me to the point where I don't let difficulties or huge numbers scare me because of my present situation. I may not have what is needed at the moment, but when I remember who my God is and the promises He has made to me, I won't be intimidated or lose sight of what has already been declared over my life.

Let's Talk About Movement

When it comes to movement, it is always important to remain in the proper stance, which allows you to stay alert. It is not the time to relax and get comfortable on the court. When you are in the proper stance, you can react or think ahead to play more successfully in the game. So, when it comes to the heat that life brings, you must have the proper stance of being planted and immovable. Now is not the time to slip or trip up on your own feet or anyone else's. When it seems like you are not going anywhere, or if it seems like what God has spoken over you is not coming to pass, stay planted. Another proper stance is waiting patiently. While you are diligently working, you must hold on to the promises of God. Then take on the stance of faith, knowing that you can accomplish what you were sent here to do.

Sprinting is especially important. Now is not the time for lazy running. Sprinting in the game allows you to get from point "A" to the next spot where you need to be, which is point "B." Many of you have been given the plays long ago, but you have been stagnant. It is time to sprint to where the Coach needs you to be.

Many of us have been in the game, moving our feet but not dribbling the ball (which is called traveling). We have been on the go doing everything else except working the things right in our hands. It is time to dribble the ball. Meaning it is time to work the ball you have been given. What has God gifted you to do? What has God given you the authority to do on the earth? Walking in authority, as defined by W. Elwell is functioning in the ability and power you have been given to complete an action. It also allows you to act without hindrance because you have been granted permission and are no longer stagnant. You are filled with greatness and with so much value. So, it is time to start living as such, for we are God's masterpieces. He has created us anew in Christ Jesus, so we can do the good things He planned for us long ago, according to Ephesians 2:10 (NLT).

Some of you may have been traveling and stopped dribbling because you were dropping dimes for other people. Which simply means you have successfully assisted others to score. You have helped people get to their goals, purpose, and destiny. Nothing is wrong with that, but when you lose focus on what you are called to, you must reevaluate your actions. Teamwork is a beautiful thing. I don't believe we are to get to where we are going alone. We need help. So, as you are assisting other people, make sure you are surrounded by people who understand the plays that are specific to you so they can drop dimes to aid you in scoring also.

You might have been just playing in the game with no real direction—thinking you knew what you were doing, but just throwing shots up, bricking every time. What you tried never went into the basket. God wants you to take time out and listen to Him, the Coach, to find out how you need to play at this point. He will give the right plays for where you are in life right now, so when He puts you back in, you can regroup and swish!

Now take a moment to reflect...

What type of movement do you need to work on in this season of your life?

_____

_____

_____

_____

_____

_____

_____

_____

_____

_____

Chapter Six
GOOD GAME

At the end of every game, I like to see when each team acknowledges the other for a game well played. The players slap fives and say, "Good game." I desire to play well with each day I am given. Despite what I may face or what may try to trample me down, I want the end result to be that I played well. I want the same for you. I want you to play well by giving all and living to full capacity. This game of life can throw many curve balls, but even in the midst of that, we must still heed the call—the purpose for which we were placed on this earth. So when the pressure comes, and the temperature rises, don't let it phase you. With all that you have before you, do everything as unto the Lord. Please keep moving, hustling, and driving because this game will eventually end. When it is all said and done, I want our heavenly Father (Coach) to be well pleased with how well we took the playbook (Bible) and lived by it. I want Him to be pleased with every movement we perform on the earth. I want everyone to hear those beautiful words, "Well done, good and faithful servant." So, what are you doing with what you have been given? God has graced us with great skill and ability to serve and be impactful to fulfill our kingdom assignment. So, the question is, have you been faithful over what you have been given?

Pivot past the distractions that cause you to lose focus. Pivot past the hindrances that come to block you. Pivot past the enemy that tries to sabotage the very gifts God has given you by implanting your thoughts with lies to make you fearful of moving. I speak movement over you. Take the ball in your hand, move your feet, and dribble down the path God has lit up for you. You making it down that path is not for you and you alone but for those assigned to you so that their lives can be forever changed. Hallelujah!

My Prayer

Father, I pray over this reader that was drawn to this book. I pray that they have been blessed with the words poured from my heart. I pray that they will diligently work the very things that You placed in their hands. I ask that You give them the strength to stand and persevere in heated situations that came to hinder, or block them and to test their endurance and faith in You. God, I ask that You be pleased with their diligence, determination, and dedication as they position themselves to fulfill what You have placed in them so that they can be impactful in the earth—all for You to be glorified. Father, I pray that as they place You at the center of their lives, You will align them to bring balance in every area and that nothing will be lacking. I pray that movement will begin to happen in their lives in the places where they have been stagnant. Father, please remind them again of who they are in You and what You have spoken over them. I pray they will trust You with their lives, for You are a God that does not lie. Whatever their hands find to do, I pray it will be unto You. Father, please bless the work of their hands. Lord, let the giftings and callings placed within them be awakened and come forth because the time is now. I pray their ears are open to Your voice, to hear Your instructions that will lead them on the path they are to go, to lean not unto their own understanding but trust You wholeheartedly. I pray their eyes open to see that there is more to them, and to see the greatness that is within them. I ask this in Jesus' name, Amen!

References

What Are Some Characteristics of Diligent People?, https://www.reference.com/world-view/characteristics-diligent-people-b3c41b7de82c52cb. Accessed 10 August 2022.

"DILIGENCE | definition in the Cambridge English Dictionary." Cambridge Dictionary, 8 March 2022, https://dictionary.cambridge.org/us/dictionary/english/diligence. Accessed 14 March 2023.

Elwell, Walter A. "Authority in the Bible - Definition, Meaning and References." Bible Study Tools, https://www.biblestudytools.com/dictionary/authority/. Accessed 23 September 2022.

Hawk, Greg. "Basketball Terminology." Linn-Benton Community College, https://cf.linnbenton.edu/mathsci/math/lewisr/web.cfm?pgID=3612. Accessed 14 March 2022.

"heat*ing up What Is Heating Up In Basketball? Definition & Meaning On SportsLingo." SportsLingo, https://www.sportslingo.com/sports-glossary/h/heating-up/. Accessed 3 March 2022.

"Hope Definition & Meaning." Merriam-Webster, https://www.merriam-webster.com/dictionary/hope. Accessed 3 March 2023.

"Impactful Definition & Meaning." Merriam-Webster, https://www.merriam-webster.com/dictionary/impactful. Accessed 4 July 2022.

"Know the difference between fake hustle and good hustle in basketball." Basketball Society, 28 April 2017, https://basketballsocietyonline.com/know-difference-fake-hustle-good-hustle-basketball. Accessed 3 March 2022.

"Tetralogy of Fallot - Symptoms and causes." Mayo Clinic, 17 August 2021, https://www.mayoclinic.org/diseases-conditions/tetralogy-of-fallot/symptoms-causes/syc-20353477. Accessed 21 November 2021.

"Trust Definition & Meaning." Merriam-Webster, https://www.merriam-webster.com/dictionary/trust. Accessed 14 September 2022.

BIOGRAPHY

Alissia Miles is a psalmist, writer, preacher, wife, and mother, among other things. As a daughter of a pastor, Alissia knows about the variety of needs that face ministry for both those a part of and in need of it. She is never one to settle with just checking the box of coming to services; she strives to continuously encounter the presence of God with every note sung or message preached, and she makes sure that everyone in the vicinity comes along with her. Alissia has a passion for young girls and works to help them learn lessons to become godly women through teaching and mentorship in a program she developed called God's Beautiful Girls (GBG). Alissia graduated from the University of Phoenix in 2014 with a degree in Business Management. Alissia has been happily married since 2006 to her husband, Tyshawn Miles. They have four children and currently reside in Dallas, Texas.

Made in the USA
Monee, IL
22 December 2023

48264331R00037